The Prospecting Survival Guide Vol. 2 - Advanced Strategies

From the
SURVIVE
TO THRIVE®
Training Series

By Jay Maymi
(Author of "Survive to Thrive" – A Practical Guide for the New Network Marketer

Copyright © 2017 by Jay Maymi

ISBN 978-0-9915419-4-2

All rights reserved. No part of this book may be used or reproduced by any means, graphic, electronic, or mechanical, including photocopying, recording, taping or by any information storage retrieval system without the written permission of the publisher except in the case of brief quotations embodied in critical articles and reviews.

Because of the dynamic nature of the Internet, any web addresses or links contained in this book may have changed since publication and may no longer be valid. The views expressed in this work are solely those of the author and do not necessarily reflect the views of the publisher, and the publisher hereby disclaims any responsibility for them.

Any people depicted in stock imagery provided by iStock Photo are models, and such images are being used for illustrative purposes only. Certain stock imagery © iStock Photo.

The Prospecting Survival Guide Vol. 2 - Advanced Strategies

From the
SURVIVE TO THRIVE®
Training Series

PREFACE

Welcome to the Prospecting Survival Guide Vol. II: Advanced Strategies (PSG II). Let me put it bluntly - you hold in your hand the prospecting tool to turn it all around. I mean it. This training resource is yet another excuse eliminator as to why your prospecting is not where you know it should or needs to be. The good news is that your business is about to change if you are willing to do the work. If you are familiar with the first Prospecting Survival Guide (if you are not then I would highly recommend that you pick that copy up as well), you already know that in it I provide 22 incredible, unique, and some even funny ways to create your own prospecting playbook. Well, this book adds a few more to the pile. The difference with these new ones is that they are advanced and will demand that you UP your prospecting approach and disciplines. In other words, due to the advanced and technical nature of these strategies you must be confident in what you are doing. The original PSG provided prospecting ideas that anyone at any level can implement and begin to develop their prospecting muscles and increase activity.

THE PROSPECTING SURVIVAL GUIDE, VOL. 2

It was a novice approach, yet incredibly effective. PSG II takes it to a level of mastery.

Finally, let me just remind you what prospecting ultimately is and is not. Prospecting is not searching, seeking, or hunting for people that will join you in business or do business with you. This is a terrible misconception that leads to tremendous confusion and quick discouragement when the desired results are not experienced. Prospecting is simply the art of finding people that will give you some of their time. Period. Once they have given you the time you requested, and they have seen what you have to offer, then they'll decide whether to join or buy based on several factors such as the effectiveness of the presentation, the quality of information, and their own personal situation. However, none of that is relevant if you never find the prospect who will give you time. Does this make sense to you so far? All heads nodding...YES!

To your prospecting success,

Jay Maymi

INTRODUCTION

If you are reading this Guide then you are someone who seeks to grow their business not only through personal self-development, motivation, and inspiration but also through the continuing development of your business skills and knowledge. Any serious entrepreneur who values technical improvement as well as creating a clear accomplishment distance between themselves and the next entrepreneur will constantly pursue the information available and necessary to give him or her that winning edge. This Guide will do exactly that for you. In my personal pursuit of creative and exciting ways to find new prospects, I have discovered a few more ways that have added another layer of prospecting techniques to incorporate into my personal prospecting playbook. These prospecting strategies that I am going to share with you have all worked to one extent or another. Some have worked more often than others and those that have worked less frequently have produced greater results when they did work. The fact is that there is no rhyme or reason to the success of each of these strategies. Bottom line is that they will work for you because they have worked for me and others whom I've taught them to and who have utilized them as well. My strong recommendation is to study each of the strategies first and then create an action plan around them. As in any effort that is worthwhile, you must have a meticulous game plan before you begin. That being said...LET THE PROSPECTING PARTY COMMENCE!

THE PROSPECTING SURVIVAL GUIDE, VOL. 2

ADVANCED STRATEGY #1

WARN REPORT (or WARN NOTICE)

For this strategy to be fully appreciated you must first understand the WARN ACT. The WARN (Worker Adjustment Retraining Notification) Act is federal legislation that offers protection to workers affected by an upcoming layoff or business closing. It requires employers to provide notice 60 days in advance of any closing or layoff to the U.S. Department of Labor who is responsible for the enforcement of this Act. As such, every state DOL must produce a monthly WARN REPORT or NOTICE to inform the public of the pending layoffs or business closings. This is public information that can be found on many state DOL websites by simply searching WARN REPORT and then your state. For example, search WARN Report NY (see fig.1). Or, you can go to www.layofflist.org for a quicker search (see fig.2). Not all states have WARN reports, but many do. If your state does not, then you'll have a little more homework to do in locating the report. You can call the DOL to inquire at (202)219-5577. Whichever way you arrive at accessing this valuable information it will prove absolute GOLD for you.

THE PROSPECTING SURVIVAL GUIDE, VOL. 2

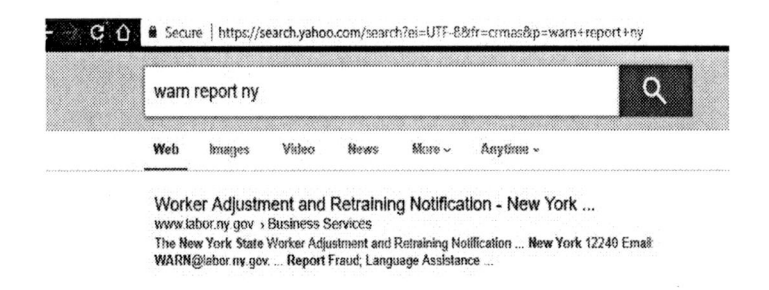

Figure 1

Figure 2

Now, I can almost see many of you salivating right now. I can now envision a stunned look with eyes wide open while a slow dribble pours from the side of your mouth due to your jaw hanging so low to your waist in amazement. Am I right? I know the look because that was me when I first discovered this strategy. Once you gather yourselves, I know the questions will be "who, what, where, how, etc." Hang in there because I'm going to break it all down.

THE PROSPECTING SURVIVAL GUIDE, VOL. 2

First, once you locate the WARN Report, you are looking for 3 bits of information. Just keep in mind that not all state WARN Reports are the same. However, they all provide the essential information you will need in order to have a great shot at success with this strategy. This information is the company or business who is closing or laying off, the amount of people affected, and location of business. Some may even provide the name of the person either in the HR department or another point of contact who is the person you will be contacting. In NY, all the critical information is already provided on the report. If your report does not provide the contact person, then don't fret. It is fairly simple to locate either the HR person or Manager by simply searching the company online, calling them, and asking them who is responsible for reporting layoffs to the DOL. They will provide that information to you. Additionally, some state DOL sites are not as user friendly as others but be diligent in scouring the site and you'll find the report. *(To arrive at the page below, click the "Resources" tab at the top of fig. 2 and then click on the desired state).*

THE PROSPECTING SURVIVAL GUIDE, VOL. 2

The next step is to contact the individual who you located as the contact person for the company. This individual is the one responsible for providing the information to the DOL regarding the layoff or closing. They are your point of contact and the person who will ultimately make the final decision on your proposal.

Figure 3

ITS VERY IMPORTANT TO UNDERSTAND THIS...

The main purpose of contacting this individual is to offer them a value-added opportunity to expose their incumbent workers a chance to explore other careers and industries, develop new skills and social media and resume improvement skills. This is accomplished by holding an on-site workshop. The goal for most HR personnel or someone of the like is to provide their incumbent workers as best a chance to re-enter the workforce as quickly as possible. This means that they would be open to workshops or training sessions that can up-skill their soon to be laid off employees. This is where this Advanced Strategy begins to unfold. When you make contact, the key is to stress to them that you would like to provide their employees a workshop for career development. Below is a script that works very well.

A few final critical points:

1.) The HR Personnel or Managers sometimes get called upon by other financial companies soliciting their employees for rollover business because they too are aware of the WARN Report. So, they may have their "guards up" when you call. However, the minute you mention worker training, workforce re-entry, or employer career development they tend to be very open to the conversation.

2.) You cannot state that you are hiring for your company or are recruiting for your company. This is not the purpose for your call or intent. Your initial intent is about education and awareness that can empower and equip a laid off person to find a new career opportunity. This is what will allow you access to establish an onsite workshop.

3.) You must create a value-added workshop which will require you to reach out to resume writing experts, social media job hunting experts, etc.

4.) Your topic in this workshop will not be about your company and should not be your company presentation but a generic approach to different careers and industries that are in demand of new talent such as financial services. Do you get the picture, here?

5.) When you create a proposal letter you must create it with general career information and not just your business on it.

Lastly, the initial call is everything. The words are everything. This is where you'll make it or break it. If you can get past the initial few seconds and engage your contact with your idea, then you will be on your way. I have provided a script below that has worked extremely well.

"Hello, can I speak with_____? My name is Jay Maymi and I was calling because your company is listed on the WARN Report for closure on____ __ and affecting_____employees. (Wait for acknowledgement). I work with associates that provide soon to be laid off workers with information and education on new career opportunities, growing industries, resume writing, improved social media job searching skills, and many additional resources to equip them for a faster and better re-entry into the workforce. Is this something that your employees can

benefit from?"

The typical response that I have received is yes. This is followed by a question as to the cost. I answer that there is no cost to anyone and its part of equipping laid off personnel. When they ask, who do I represent I answer that I have my own independent firm working with many companies who are always looking for new talent. Which is true, right?

FINAL POINTS

1.) Expect them to ask you to send them information.

2.) Expect them to get back to you quickly because they are working against the clock. They only have a certain amount of time before closing.

3.) Make sure that you can assemble other value-added service professionals for your group workshop.

4.) Focus on the smaller companies (less than 50 employees). The bigger the company the harder the task. My success has been with companies with less than 35 layoffs.

5.) Finally, some of my biggest rollover accounts have been because of this strategy.

Good Luck!

THE PROSPECTING SURVIVAL GUIDE, VOL. 2

ADVANCED STRATEGY #2

MYOPPORTUNITY.COM

Figure 4

What is My Opportunity? This is a lead generation tool built inside of a business network. This service is almost like an online business and professional match maker. They match you with candidates that match well with the profile and filter search that you create. I started using this strategy about a year ago and it has proven to be a fantastic prospecting resource for those with advanced communication skills. The reason why I say advanced skills is because of the nature of the site and the caliber of prospects that this prospecting gem will deliver. This strategy is one that can really pile on prospects at your fingertips within an instant and continue to do so, almost daily. Crazy, I know! Below are the steps to this beauty.

THE PROSPECTING SURVIVAL GUIDE, VOL. 2

First, you sign up at MyOpportunity.com as a Hiring Manager (see fig.4). This is important because many make the mistake of signing up as a Job Seeker or Networker and as a result do not see this work out for them as it should. Additionally, you will have to pay a small monthly subscription fee, but it is well worth it, which you will agree almost immediately after seeing your first few hundred "Leads" appear in your inbox.

The next step is critical. You need to set up your profile and filters based on the types of other profiles that would match well with your search. So, as a seeker of talent (Hiring Manager), make sure to set your hiring manager search with skill sets, industries, related experience that match well with your business or company opportunity (see fig.5). Additionally, make sure to cast a wide net, not only with the type of person you're looking for but also in the areas of the country as well.

CAUTION! Do not open yourself to receive matches or "leads" in an area of the country that strong company support, leadership, or offices are non-existent. This is a formula for disaster and everyone's

THE PROSPECTING SURVIVAL GUIDE, VOL. 2

time being wasted. I have experienced that already. I now set my profile for matches that are within the tri-state area of NY. This has worked out much better. The cool aspect of this strategy is that you can wake up every day and your MyOpportunity inbox is loaded with brand new prospects. So, as opposed to running around prospecting outdoors, at the mall, and talking to strangers that you know nothing about, here's a way to meet people who have already declared that they are seeking new opportunities plus have provided you with a little insight on themselves. Isn't that somethin'?

By the way, I know what many of you are thinking. You're thinking that you don't hire people for a job opportunity and what you offer is opportunity of employment through self-employment, so how do I tackle this pre-conceived job opportunity mindset that these leads will have? Let me answer that by first saying to you **GET OUT OF YOUR OWN HEAD.** Stop overthinking or overanalyzing what you think other people are thinking about what they want. You don't know that and never will until you speak to them.

THE PROSPECTING SURVIVAL GUIDE, VOL. 2

That being said, you are not incorrect about the pre-conceived notion that many on this site are looking for a standard job opportunity, however, many are just looking for opportunity no matter how it's dressed up. Got it?

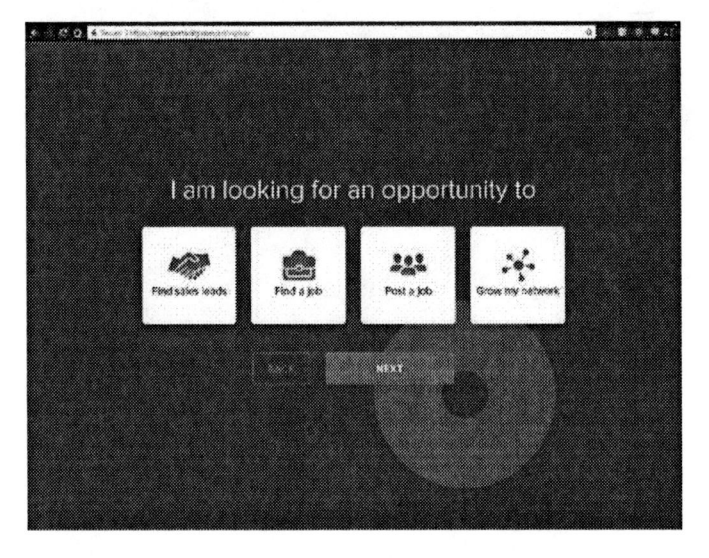

Figure 5

The key, however, is how you word your initial "job" posting and hence how you make the initial contact with your new lead. This is where you can clarify your position and what your company does and is looking for in new talent. I will provide below a few different email messages that I use which does exactly this - clarify the reason for me reaching out to them and the opportunity as well. Quite frankly, if I do say so myself as a subject matter expert...this is pure word symphony.

Before I share the email content scripts that you would send to your inbox leads let me just point out that the follow-up for any lead who is interested in further information will be determined by whatever method of information and opportunity sharing you are most comfortable doing. For the record, I don't believe nor practice sending out videos or website links or anything of the like. I'm not opposed to doing such things but only after I have had a chance to speak with them myself and they have had a chance to hear my voice and passion for what I do. This is critical because people join you first, then your cause or business. I have experienced tremendous success in recruiting people simply because we have hit it off on the phone. Remember that YOU are the first and foremost effective recruiting tool you have at your disposal ALWAYS!

THE PROSPECTING SURVIVAL GUIDE, VOL. 2

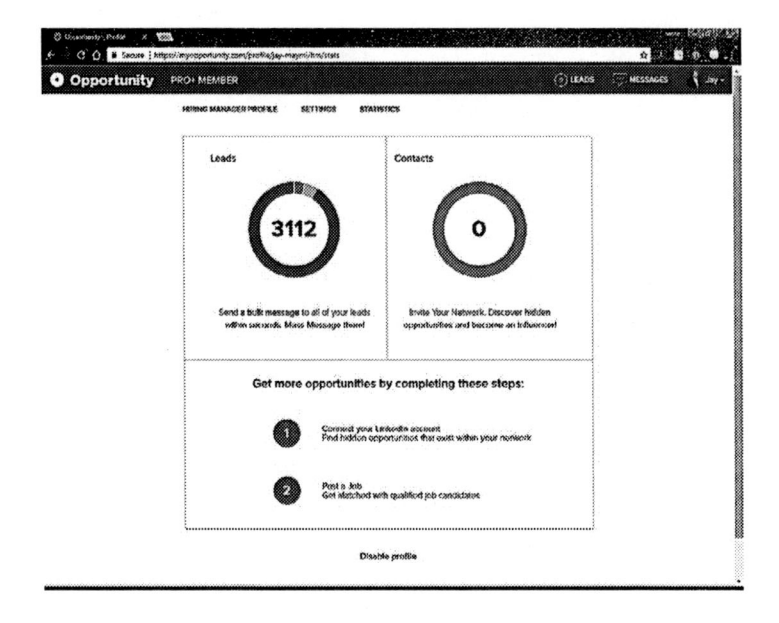

Figure 6

The rest is magic, folks. As you begin to have leads in your inbox daily you can decipher who you want to reach out to with any of the email content scripts below. I've learned that some leads are not worth reaching out but overall most are. All you can do is send the email and wait for the response that you will predictably and inevitably get. Go for it!

Email Content (4 different versions)

"_____, my name is Jay Maymi. After reviewing your profile, I'm interested in speaking with you regarding independent work opportunities with our financial company. Our company has been spearheading financial literacy, education, and awareness for three decades. Due to expansion, the interest in meeting entrepreneurial- minded sales professionals have increased. If you are keeping your options open for a rewarding and meaningful professional career experience (whether F/T, P/T, or flexible Twin Career) with the potential to change lives, then we should speak about our range of involvement possibilities. We have an excellent training program, leadership incentives, tremendous growth potential, and an outstanding compensation platform. It's worth a brief chat."

"_____, my name is Jay Maymi. After reviewing your profile, even though, your experience is not specifically compatible, I'm still very interested in speaking with you regarding entrepreneurial opportunities with our financial company. Our company has been spearheading financial literacy, education, and awareness for three decades. Due to demand, our interest in meeting diversified, quality professionals have increased. If you are keeping your options open for a career experience (whether F/T, P/T, or flexible Twin Career) with the potential to change lives, then we should speak about our range of involvement possibilities. We have an excellent training program, leadership incentives, tremendous growth potential, and an outstanding compensation platform. It's worth a brief chat."

"_____, my name is Jay Maymi and based on the industries that you have worked in PLUS your skill set, I am interested in speaking with you regarding our current expansion plans in your area as well as career opportunities with our financial company. We have a sales mentoring / management career opportunity that matches well with your past experiences. We offer flexibility, unlimited income potential, residual and renewal compensation, ownership, training and support, plus a highly successful marketing campaign. If you are keeping your options open then let's discuss our company, financial literacy and awareness initiatives, compensation, and overall opportunity in greater detail. We can also discuss the flexible part time/twin career option as well."

Hello, _____. My name is Jay Maymi. I wanted to reach out because Opportunity highly matched your profile score to my search. I noticed your work-related experience in Sales Management, Sales, Business Development as well as read your Bio. As a result, I would be interested in speaking with you regarding our company's current expansion plans, our mission to help reduce the financial illiteracy rate in this country, and finally our sales, management, and entrepreneurial leadership opportunities. I realize that this may not be exactly the opportunity you're pursuing, however, if you are willing to keep an open mind then our company, initiatives, mission, and compensation structure may intrigue you further. We can also speak about Part Time and Independent Contractor opportunity.

Good Luck!

THE PROSPECTING SURVIVAL GUIDE, VOL. 2

ADVANCED STRATEGY #3

NON-LICENSING PROSPECTING WITH NETLAW AND BOLT INSURANCE

I've noticed that some of the best tools that we have to prospect with for new associates are the least utilized tools by Associates. It has baffled me that with such easy products to market due to the non-license requirement and the referral structure of them that more Associates are not using these services as great prospecting strategies. The two services that I believe are incredible for prospecting new recruits are NetLaw and Bolt. I have had a field day with these services as a way to become very creative in prospecting. Just imagine building an army of Associates who only market NetLaw and Bolt and you get to cross-sell their clients. I know. The possibilities are extremely exciting, right? The incredible part is that at any time these Associates can decide to fully engage in the opportunity and get licensed. Well, before I dive into the actual prospecting strategies of each, let me list key reasons why they are a no brainer and worthy of adding to your prospecting playbook.

1.) As I mentioned, there is no licensing required which means that anybody who joins can start making money the very next day. Think about it. Isn't this what people want? Absolutely. A prospect who feels that they can start generating income 24 hours from the minute they sign up will be more apt to join than someone who realizes that their ability to generate an income may come in a few weeks to a month, possibly. It's crazy not to leverage this, folks.

2.) There really is no language barrier to market these products. Why? They sell themselves! How much English do you need to speak to understand that in the U.S. you need to have car insurance? It's the law. I mean, really. This opens a gateway of recruiting possibilities like I've never seen. Everybody knows someone who has a car and has car insurance. Or a business, a home, a pet, an apartment, or is self-employed. With NetLaw, anybody can ask a few questions to their market of contact, send out a very brief text message embedded with the NetLaw 3-minute video, and register their prospect for the service on an app.

Anyone can do this as well if you are asking the right prospect.

3.) These are services that people already need whether you joined the business or not. Whether it is a Property Casualty product or a Will and Estate Planning service, most Americans either need or are looking for these services. Unlike insurance or investments, you don't have to "convince" a client of the importance of doing it. Even with having a Will, most people know they should have one but don't due to a variety of factors, i.e. cost, confusion, time involved, etc.

4.) Lastly, there is hardly any real training needed. Certainly, some training is necessary, but it is not time consuming and there is no studying involved.

5.) There is a low barrier of entry when considering a new prospect's intelligence or academic capabilities to process higher level learning and the more complex aspects of our business.

netlaw

NETLAW

When considering building an army of NetLaw-focused Associates, you should take time to really think who would be great candidates that can offer NetLaw as a value-added service. These are prospects that already offer a service which has a synergistic relationship with Will and Estate Planning Services. In other words, having a conversation about the establishment of a Will and Estate Plan would not be a foreign topic for them to introduce to their clients. I have current Associates in my organization that I introduced the NetLaw opportunity concept to who had been looking at the time for additional services to offer their clients that made sense. Ultimately, here is the key. **Pay attention.** Service professionals and product providing entrepreneurs are the ones most open to multiple sources of income ONLY if it makes strategic business sense to them. Did you get that? I hope so because in there are the seeds to a great recruiting conversation and question. Do you see it? Below is a list of these excellent prospects to speak to regarding the NetLaw opportunity:

Realtors, Property Casualty Agents, Tax Professionals, Mortgage Professionals, Attorneys, Title Agents, Notary Public, Health Insurance Agents, and Life Insurance Agents.

Script

"Julie, based on what you do as a_____, if you could provide another value-added service that makes sense for your clients to have and compliments what you do for them would you be open to that brief discussion? (WFA) Great. Most clients you work with don't have a Will or Estate Plan but are looking to establish one. If you could educate them by showing them a brief video, answering a few questions, and then helping them get the work done, they would do it and you'd get paid for registering them for the service. Look, some things are better seen to be understood. Let me send you the 3-minute video that our company, NetLaw, has created to educate people about having a Will and an Estate Plan. This is what your clients would need to see first. The rest is easy and simple to do by you. Make sure to watch it. I'll follow up within the hour."

Professional service providers and entrepreneurs are not the only ones who are appealing prospects to approach with the NetLaw opportunity. In fact, right under your nose you have access to a few prospects with tremendous potential to become advocates of NetLaw's services. These are people that have great potential either because of their current occupations, social influence, and/or unique situation.

Additionally, the appeal of earning extra income on a flexible basis also makes for a worthwhile feature to present. Below are wonderful prospects worth pursuing.

Pastors:
They are incredible centers of influence and would totally get behind an awareness cause like having a Will and Estate Plan. Pastors are big proponents of financial preparedness.

Existing clients:
This one is a gem and completely overlooked. While many clients will not have an interest in the licensing aspect of our opportunity (hence, why they don't join) they would be open to earning extra income by sharing the NetLaw information to their friends, family, co-workers, etc. I mean, really, how much work is involved in sending out a 3-minute NetLaw video and then helping someone get registered for the service? Not much work at all. However, if you don't take a few minutes to show them how easy it is they will never know what could have become for them a great source of meaningful part time income.

At-home mom:
What do many at home moms want? They want what an opportunity like what WFG / NetLaw offers - flexibility of involvement, freedom to choose, work from home accommodations, income earning potential, ability to raise their children, a non-hectic and stressful opportunity that does not require a ton of commitment to learn. If you speak to at-home moms with these terms and then introduce how they

can achieve what they want as a WFG/NetLaw Associate, you will find your team will grow with a powerful group of people.

Law Enforcement and Firefighters:
Some of my best Associates have been those in law enforcement and firefighting because they truly understand the value of having a Will and all the proper family legal documents in order. These awesome people are, not only, advocates of having a Will but are also very credible sources to campaign on behalf of NetLaw. Finally, I've not met one person in either occupation who was against earning extra income.

Script
"Hey, Alan. I am an advocate for educating people about the importance of having a Will and an Estate Plan in place. I do this by simply sharing with my community a brief awareness video, answer a few questions, and then refer them to my company for the next step. They pay me to do this. Considering what you do and the quality person you are, I think you'd be an excellent addition to the

company as an advocate as well. (WFA) Let me do this so that you are better informed. I'll send you the 3-minute client awareness video so you can see for yourself how we educate on the topic of having a Will and Estate Plan. I'll follow up with you in an hour or so and explain the rest. It's a pretty easy and simple way to pick up additional income by doing something meaningful for people."

Send the video via text. Why? You want to begin showing them how easy it is to do the business. When you speak with them highlight the importance of having a Will, the fact that people need and are looking to get them done, and how they can earn an additional $1,000 a month by registering 7 new NetLaw clients in a month at an Associate level. I like to say to them that they get paid $142.11 for about 10 minutes' worth of work. This is what an Associate earns for every sale. Got it?

Closing Point - MAKE IT EASY ON YOURSELF. USE THE NETLAW VIDEO. IT DOES ALL THE WORK. IT IS AN EXCELLENT MARKETING PIECE FOR NETLAW RECRUITING AND SELLING.

BOLT

If there was ever a "no-brainer" prospecting tool for recruiting new Associates, BOLT is it. Unfortunately, because many existing Associates are not terribly familiar with the world of Property and Casualty (it's a foreign language to them) there continues to be missed opportunities for picking up new teammates in droves. Think about it for a second. What is the one product or service that millions of people in the U.S. must have if they want the privilege of driving a car? What is a must for all homeowners? What is highly recommended for business owners of all types? The answers are obvious - auto, home, and liability insurance. Here is the next question. What is it that most people shop often and have no loyalty to? Yep. Their auto insurance. So, what I just spoke about is the tremendous leverage that, as an entrepreneur, you can have. In this case, a product that millions are required to have, a product that people are open to explore better value elsewhere, and that they have very little loyalty to their providing company. Add to this that there is no licensing required, no major devotion to study or product know how, flexibility of involvement, and a simple 1-minute process to get a brand-new client started, and what you have is a prospecting **GOLDMINE** for recruiting an army of Bolt referring agents.

So, who would also be "no-brainer" to prospect for that would make great (and easy) candidates to speak to about the WFG/BOLT opportunity? Those that are already able to assimilate the BOLT conversation because of what they already do. Let me give you some obvious examples and some not so obvious.

Car Salesman (whether independent, a used lot, or dealership) - They all make great prospects to talk to about offering their customers auto insurance. They have a captive customer when they are selling a car. Once you show them how easy the process is, it becomes very difficult to say no to joining the WFG/ BOLT opportunity. One of the top referring Associates in BOLT is a Toyota Car Salesman that I recruited with this exact approach.

Group Health Benefits Representatives / Aflac - They deal with business owners all day long and business owners usually carry Commercial Liability insurance. They are already talking to the business owners anyway.

Mortgage and Realtors - Yet, another obvious one. Who better to discuss homeowner insurance than the Realtor who is about to close on a house sale? Or, the Loan Officers who deal with buyers that need homeowner's insurance before they close?

These are more "outside the box" prospecting for potential WFG/BOLT recruits:

Auto Repair Shops (start with the one you get your car fixed at). I recently spoke to my mechanic and proposed the opportunity to offer BOLT auto quotes from his very busy shop and he was all in. He is in the process of getting a banner made for his shop.

THE PROSPECTING SURVIVAL GUIDE, VOL. 2

Beverage Salesman, Beer, or Route Delivery Person - they deliver to grocery stores, restaurants, pizzerias, etc. This is perfect for Commercial Liability or BOP's.

Owners or Managers of Pet Stores, Animal Hospitals, or Dog Grooming Salons - BOLT offers Pet Insurance.... need I say more?

At-Home Moms, Travel Agencies, Immigration offices, Driving Schools, Tax Preparers / Accountants, Boat Yards, Motorcycle Sales and Repair Shops, Health Insurance Agents, Retired Baby Boomers, Independent Life Insurance Agents

Script
The script here is flexible because of the many ways to prospect for new recruits. It all depends on the person you are approaching. So, what's important is the story of who you are, what you do (with respect to a BOLT referring agent), and then connecting the dots for them. Here is an example:

"_____, I'm an expansion rep for a major national insurance agency called BOLT Insurance and they have set up an affiliate referral program to pay those who have a business where BOLT can set up a referral site. This means that because BOLT offers Pet Insurance having a referral site in your Pet Store or Dog Grooming Shop would be ideal. For example... (give them a solid example until they connect the dots)."

WARNING! Do not proceed until they get it. They must have the "aha moment." Some will and some won't. I have recruited an owner of a local pet store with this approach. He does about 2 policies a week. It's not much but slowly he's starting to see an opportunity in it.

FINAL POINTS

The key to successful prospecting and recruiting in this strategy is to keep it simple. The appeal is that it is a non-complicated and non- time-consuming way to generate another $1,000 a month by referring clients for services that people either already have or need to have. You will have a measure of solid recruiting success if you propose to your prospects that the WFG BOLT and NetLaw income earning opportunity is a seamless way to generate another source of income without distraction.

Secondly, this is an excellent way to have another person (or group) fill up your client prospecting list with potential cross-over sales. Think about it. Your new Associate who just registered a client for NetLaw has just added a prospect for you to follow up with to set up a client meeting. The same goes for any new BOLT customer or quoted Invite.

Lastly, you truly shoot yourself in the business foot by not incorporating these two services into your Prospecting Playbook (see Prospecting Survival Guide Vol. I).

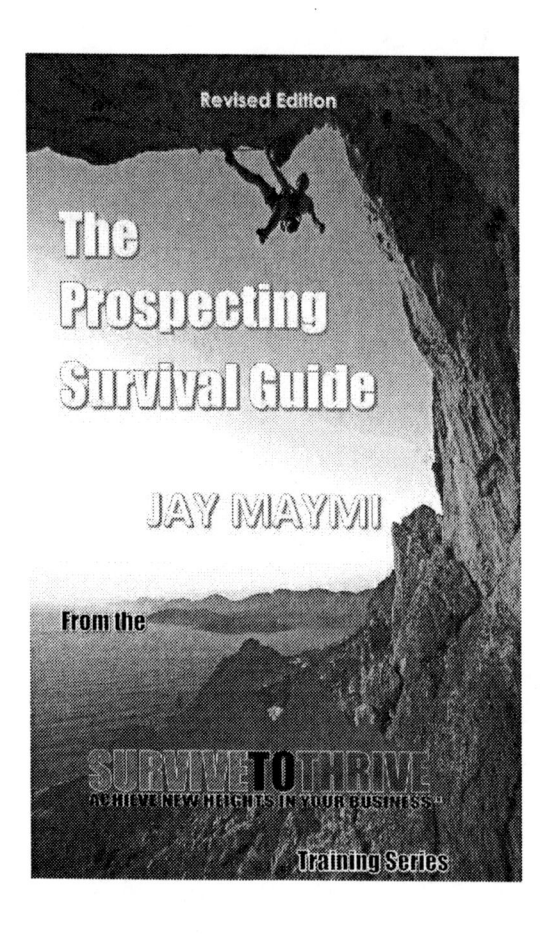

THE PROSPECTING SURVIVAL GUIDE, VOL. 2

ADVANCED STRATEGY #4

LINKEDIN ADVANCED SEARCHES

If you have read the first Prospecting Survival Guide, then you'll know that LinkedIn is an absolute gem for finding people right at your fingertips. There are incredible prospecting opportunities on there if you know how to use them. In the last two years, I have discovered how to find even more prospects by maximizing the search feature on LinkedIn (see fig.7). In this next section, what I will do is provide very effective new searches. I will not, however, rehash what I have already covered in the first PSG as well as the Bootcamps, i.e. creating an attractive profile, the magic of the search bar, utilizing the filters, connecting email scripts, etc. I will provide the email content that is most attractive and appropriate for each of the new searches. Finally, let me reiterate that a key component to the success of this strategy is in the follow up and your ability to create enough fascination and intrigue that it leads to the action of an appointment with your prospect. Let's get started!

Figure 7

NEW SEARCHES WITH EMAIL CONTENT

Tax Franchises Search i.e., H&R Block, Liberty Tax, Jackson Hewitt, etc.

"Hi, _____. I noticed in your profile that you are currently a tax professional with_____. I'd like to speak with you regarding your career plans now that this current tax season has ended. If are keeping your professional career options open, then please let me know. I'd like to discuss our independent and flexible, financial management and financial literacy consulting opportunities with you."

Tax Preparer / CPA / Tax Professional

"_____thanks for connecting. I wanted to reach because of your CPA / Tax Preparer / Tax Professional designation (pick whichever is on their profile). Just out of curiosity, would you keep an open mind to the possibility of expanding and diversifying your tax consulting practice to include financial management or financial advisory work? You probably already know (because it really is no surprise) that a lot of tax professionals are going the route of Financial Advisor as a means of generating additional layers of current income and residual / passive income to their bottom line. Well, let me know if this is an exploratory discussion that you'd like to have."

At-Home Mom

"Hi,_____. Thanks for connecting. I noticed that you are an at home mom with solid career and professional experience, so I thought that reaching out to you would make sense. Just out of curiosity, would you be open to a discussion regarding a flexible and accommodating independent career opportunity with our financial literacy based firm? If you are currently open to such a discussion, then please reach out to me at your earliest convenience. I would love to share with you our current financial education and awareness initiatives."

A financial professional employee

"_____. thanks for connecting. I noticed that you have financial experience, so I thought that reaching out to you would make sense. I was interested in speaking with you regarding our flexible and accommodating independent consulting career opportunities with our financial literacy inspired firm. If you are currently open to such a discussion, then please reach out to me at your earliest convenience. We have a grand number of colleagues with similar backgrounds as yours with our company who are experiencing a very rewarding second professional career. I look forward to hearing from you."

A financial sales professional already with another financial company

"_____ thanks for connecting. I went over your profile and see that you have quite the experience and career in financial services. I know that you are currently with_____, but are you permanently settled there, or would you explore leadership opportunities that can capitalize on your experiences, not to mention generate an income that is not based solely on your own personal pen? If you are keeping your options open, then we should at least have a chat. Please let me know. I look forward to you reaching out."

Other insurance professionals or business owners

"_____, thanks for connecting. I looked over your profile and was interested in speaking with regarding your insurance business. There is a very good possibility that you can expand your business tremendously as an independent agent by adding a few more complimentary services to offer your clients. Those clients that are past, current, and yet to come. It may very well add a new dimension and thereby, new avenues to attract more clients. Call me so we can discuss."

Seeking employment (interchangeable with seeking new opportunities, opportunity, new career, seeking new employment)

"_____, after reviewing your profile, even though, your experience is not specifically compatible, I'm interested in speaking with you regarding entrepreneurial opportunities with our financial company. Our company has been spearheading financial literacy, education, and awareness for three decades. Due to expansion, the interest in meeting ambitious and visionary people has increased. If you are keeping your options open for a career experience (whether F/T, P/T, or flexible Twin Career) with the potential to change lives then we should speak about our range of involvement possibilities. We have an excellent training program, leadership incentives, tremendous growth potential, and an outstanding compensation platform. It's worth a brief chat."

Retired (this is a HOMERUN SEARCH)

"_____, thanks for connecting. I noticed that you are currently retired. As I reviewed your profile, I was extremely impressed with (name two work experiences) and clearly your ability to (find two notable skills, characteristics, or qualities). This is what prompted me to send you a connection request. I realize you're retired but are you open to a discussion about a **meaningful** and financially rewarding **entrepreneurial** career opportunity with **complete flexibility?** If so, I'd be happy to share our company's story and where someone of your experience could be an **impactful** addition to it. I look forward to your thoughts.

IMPORTANT NOTE

The bold words are the glamour words that make this email content so powerful *(if you are not familiar with "glamour words" then please read chapter 4 of my book Survive to Thrive)*. These are the words that ring in the ears of a retired person. Most retired people on LinkedIn would pursue an opportunity, not so much for money although that's important too, but for impact and meaningful contribution to society. Are you getting this?

THE PROSPECTING SURVIVAL GUIDE, VOL. 2

THE PROSPECTING SURVIVAL GUIDE, VOL. 2

Retired law enforcement, retired military – this search is GOLD! Retired Law enforcement and military are all about serve and protect. This is what they have dedicated their entire working career to. It is so deep in their bones that they can't just walk away from it. Therefore, they tend do so well in our industry because our mission is also to serve and protect, isn't it? Lastly, these incredible human beings are one of the most disciplined that you will ever meet. Are you starting to make the connection?

"_____, thanks for connecting. First let me say thank you for your life long career dedicated to service and protection. After viewing your profile, I was extremely impressed with (again find something to compliment) and decided to connect because our firm has a similar mission. We also believe in serving and protecting families in this country, but our weapon is financial education and financial literacy. We are looking to change lives through this mission. I realize you're retired but are you open to a discussion about a **meaningful** and financially rewarding **entrepreneurial** career opportunity with **complete**

flexibility? If so, I'd be happy to share our company's story and where someone of your experience could be an **impactful** addition to it. I look forward to your thoughts."

WOW!!! This last strategy was worth the price of the book, people! (I should have charged more...way more.)

THE PROSPECTING SURVIVAL GUIDE, VOL. 2

ADVANCED STRATEGY #5

IMMIGRATION PROSPECTING

This advance prospecting strategy is a true "outside the box" gem because it comes with a double edge - recruits and sales. Now, let me preface this segment by stating a few "**must knows**". The first is that this strategy applies to anyone regardless of nationality. It centers around the fact that we have a burgeoning application process for citizenship in the U.S. As you are aware, there are scores upon scores of undocumented immigrants and many are in the process of applying for legal status. However, the government is aware that many who are applying for legalization do so under fraudulent pretenses. One of which is claiming to be married to a U.S. citizen thereby having a greater probability in their citizenship application being approved. It is a well-documented fact that in many of these cases the "spouse" is a paid individual serving the purpose of appearing like a legitimate marriage. As a result, these are deemed phony and worthy of criminal prosecution by the USCIS. I'm sure you've seen this or have heard of this. Well, none of this is matters much to us other than serving as a great prospecting opportunity if you understand how to capitalize on it. Let's look at the sales opportunity first.

When an individual is applying for citizenship and has his or her interview scheduled with USCIS (United States Citizenship and Immigration Services) to determine citizenship approval, he or she must provide proof of life insurance with the spouse as named beneficiary. It is a requirement that must complied with. In fact, they must show up with the actual issued policy as proof. So.... can you see where this is going? How big a market is this for life insurance sales? The answer - to quote Trump - "YUUUUUGE!"

Now, here is what you must also know. There are not many insurance companies that will offer an undocumented immigrant with an expired Visa insurance coverage. However, there are one or two that I am aware of which will consider coverage, under these circumstances, as long as the applicant has filed tax returns, has a Tax ID, the original Tax ID award letter, and has a Driver's License. The potential for life sales in this area is staggering if you can begin to penetrate that community and those of influence within those precincts. Which brings me to my next point - the recruiting opportunity considering this revelation.

I recently recruited an accountant who primarily works with both demographics of immigrants - those that have attained citizenship or Green Cards and those that are undocumented. My approach was simple and straightforward. Below is what I said.

"Mr._____, I wanted to pop in because I believe that I might be able to help your undocumented immigrant tax clients improve their chances at citizenship approval. Are you currently working with any clients that are pursuing legal status? (Of course, I knew the answer already). He laughed and said, "most of them". (BINGO!) He went on to ask exactly how would I be able to help them. I continued by saying...

"We can help them by providing the life insurance policy that they are required to have to attain citizenship approval. Many companies won't provide them insurance, but I represent a company that will. (At this point came my recruit pivot question) But, let me ask you a different question. Considering that you are already their accountant and have the relationship with them, would you be open to providing that service to them right out of here? It would create another layer of soft money that you did not have before. And, I'll help you with the process." He his answer was "sure but how does it work?"

Beautiful. Absolutely beautiful.

So, who then are excellent and appropriate prospects that can see the value in "creating an additional layer of income" by offering life insurance to individuals under these circumstances? Those that would have the greatest proximity to them. In other words, those who have existing businesses or contact in communities where there is a higher concentration of immigrants.
Below is a list of these types of business or service professionals worth prospecting:

Travel Agents/Travel Agency Accountants

THE PROSPECTING SURVIVAL GUIDE, VOL. 2

Property Casualty Agents
Businesses that offer assistance with filling out Immigration forms
Immigration Attorney
Divorce Attorney Multi-Service Business
Medicaid / Medicare Representatives

These prospects are established in their respective communities and are on the front lines of working and doing business with many who would need to have life insurance for immigration purposes. The best part is that you only need one or two of them and you'll hit the jackpot.

These next 2nd tier prospects could serve as great sources of introduction to those who also have access to this immigrant community. These prospects may not be as ideal as the previously mentioned based on their current occupation or business, but they certainly are very involved with their community. In other words, they can lead you to people.

Doctors
Day Care Owners Auto Salesman
Cleaning Services Business Owners
Landscaping Business Owners

Finally, the best tactic of approach is a simple and sincere conversation. A fancy script or crafty wording is just not necessary here. The purity of the situation merits only straight talk.

Good luck!

FINRA REP OR IAR SEARCH

This strategy requires a few steps and patience but if you locate the right individual then it is very much worth it. I must reiterate that this gem is best suited for the more seasoned recruiter due to the caliber of prospects that you are pursuing. Ultimately, you are prospecting for Registered Reps and IARs who currently are not registered with a firm and are within the 2-year idle window allowed by FINRA. Reps and IAR's who are in this two-year "limbo" status often find themselves there because they are not planning on coming back to the industry, were let go from a Broker Dealer, or resigned from one. Either way, for those that are planning on staying in the industry they know that they have a two-year window to be registered otherwise they lose their FINRA registration. So, needless to say that finding who these individuals are can lead to a stockpile of ready-made securities-licensed and experienced investment professionals. These next steps will guide you through the process of finding them on FINRA, however, the method of communication you choose to contact them will vary depending on how

THE PROSPECTING SURVIVAL GUIDE, VOL. 2

resourceful you become in tracking them down. FINRA does not provide, obviously, address nor contact information but these days finding someone's address or phone number is pretty easy to do. Lastly, if you feel that you may not be very effective in having a conversation with these prospects once you locate them then find someone who will be. Let's have a look.

1.) Go to https://brokercheck.FINRA.org/
2.) In the Name or CRD# box, enter any first name of your choice, i.e. John
   and then Search (see fig. 8)

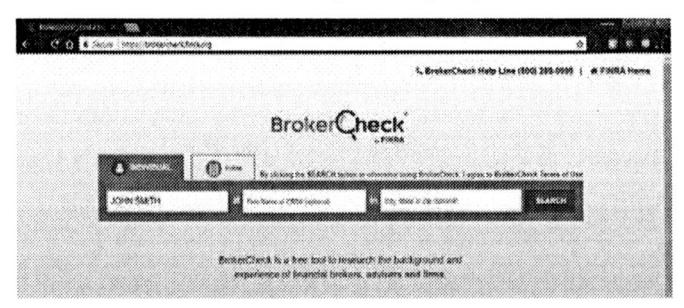

Figure 8

3.) You will find a large search appear.
4.) Click onto Show Filters (in the middle of the page – see fig. 9)

THE PROSPECTING SURVIVAL GUIDE, VOL. 2

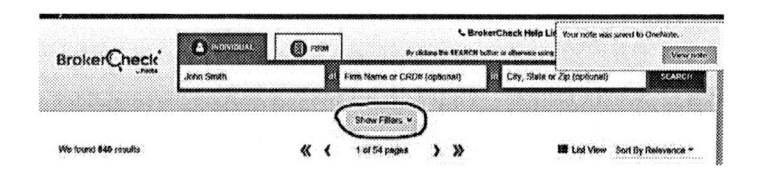

Figure 9

5.) You will see choices on how you can filter the search

6.) You want to click the following boxes TYPE – Broker; STATUS - Previously Registered and Barred; EMPLOYMENT - Include previous employers (see fig. 10).

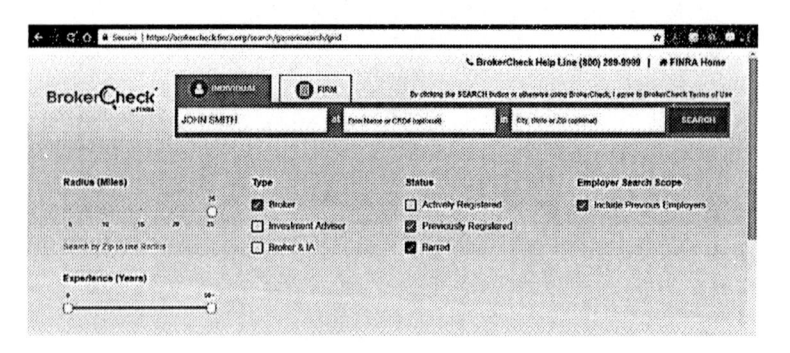

Figure 10

You will now have a massive list of Reps. This is where patience must be introduced. FINRA will not tell you specifically if the Rep is still within the two-year window. You will have to click on every Rep profile to see if they are. However, this is really no big deal. Within a second you'll know if they are or aren't still within two years. If they are then you have pretty much have everything you need. At this point, look at his or her previous employers and the city or towns where they were located. This is usually a good way to know what area (city or state) this prospect is probably from because most people tend to work within the same city/state in which they live in. Isn't this true?

From this point on, what I do is use online search engines and people locater services to help me track the phone number or address of this prospect. You do not always get a hit with this method, but it does work well enough most of the time. I have called, at times, or have sent out a letter if the phone number did not work. Keep in mind that this is another prospecting strategy that will work in many ways. The key is that you now have a way to find securities licensed people that are in transition and considering what their next step is and with what company. This is the perfect scenario in which to share the opportunity with because they are exploring their next move. Can you see the prospecting and recruiting potential for you with this method? You can really add quality financial services entrepreneurs to your organization without having to wait for the cycle of licensing. These people are out there waiting for a communication from you.

IN CLOSING

I admire each one of you who has made up their minds that good just isn't good enough. That average and ordinary just doesn't cut it for you. You understand that for you to achieve more than what you have YOU must become more than what you are. It is the shortest cut there is to success. This book, I sincerely believe, has the capacity to drastically turn your prospecting, recruiting, activity, sales, cash flow, and life around within a short amount of time. I encourage you to stay the course and stick to your dreams of building a healthy, vibrant, and thriving army of entrepreneurs and business owners. My hope is that this book doesn't become just another book or training resource that sits on your desk or in the shelf for show but that you milk it for all that it's worth. If you do then you'll be the one, one day, sharing your success story for the world to hear.

THE PROSPECTING SURVIVAL GUIDE, VOL. 2

BE SURE TO SUBSCRIBE TO THESE PORTALS FOR MORE RESOURCES AND TRAINING:

Survivetothriveguide.com

Youtube.com/JayMaymiSurvivetoThrive

Facebook.com/survivetothrivebiz

THE PROSPECTING SURVIVAL GUIDE, VOL. 2